Chapter 1.
The Debt Elephant.
"Debt means you have less to spend later"

Elephants start out small but as time goes on they grow to be huge! Debt is like an elephant that can grow bigger and bigger until it's too hard to manage. It's like having a huge weight on your chest that makes it hard to breathe. Debt can make you feel like you're not making any progress, and it can make it hard to pay for things like the food you eat. It starts with small things like a credit card, but it can grow bigger over time. Owing money can also make it hard to deal with things like losing your job. It's sort of like holding a bomb in your hands that could explode at any time.

Debt is when you owe someone else money. Interest is like a fee that you have to pay when you borrow money. When you borrow money, the person that lends you the money usually charges you some extra money (called interest) on top of what you borrowed. This is because they're letting you use their money, and they want to make some extra money too. The longer it takes you to pay back the money, the more interest you have to pay. That's why it's important to pay off your debts as soon as you can so you don't have to pay as much extra money on top!

Most kids don't usually owe too much money or have too many debts but credit cards and loans are readily available when you turn eighteen. So many eighteen to twenty year olds get themselves in debt buying things they don't really want or need.

Most people in the world owe some money to someone else. It's common for families to have debts. Most family homes are purchased with a mortgage. Some people borrow money for flashy cars and watched.Sometimes it's the feelings of worry from how much money they owe that makes people start to think more about their money and how to manage it better. That doesn't mean we have to always be worried about all types of debt though.

When we borrow money, there are two types of debt: good and bad. Good debt is when we borrow money to buy things that can help us make more money. Some people do this to start a business. We hope that the money we earn from these things will help us pay back the loan, and maybe even make extra money at the end. We don't need to worry about good debt in this part of the book. It can be risky, but there's a better chance it will work out okay. We will learn more about it later.

The other type of debt is called "bad debt". This is when you borrow money to buy something you don't really need, like a fancy car or a new phone. Buying these things can feel good at first, but it's not a smart decision if we cannot afford it. If you can't make those repayments, you'll end up owing even more money. So it's better to only borrow money for things that will make you more money in the long run. Avoid bad debt as best you can, especially when you are young.

It feels good to buy fancy things, but if you can't afford it with the money you have, it's not a good idea. This is a problem that many people have. Buying things with debt that are not necessary, like expensive sunglasses or a fancy TV.

Imagine you want to borrow money for a really cool motorbike. If you don't have enough money, you might borrow the money from your parents. Even worse, you may borrow from a dealership. Sooner or later, you will have to pay them back. This means that sometime in the future, you will have to spend your hard money on repayments. you will have less money to spend later because you'll have to give some of your weekly paycheck up to pay back that debt. This could go on for years!

So, what can we do about buying fancy things that we can't afford? Well, even really rich people still have to make choices about how they spend their money. Our goal is to help you be able to afford those fancy things, but it takes some work. At first, we need to focus on spending our money wisely, even if it's not as exciting. This might be hard, but it's important because it sets us up for a good future.

Being smart with our money means buying things that you can afford with money you currently have. We don't want to overspend if it means that we won't have any left for later. We want to make our money work for us by not wasting it on things we don't need. It's like a dog chasing its tail or a hamster running on a wheel. Instead of buying new expensive stuff now, we can buy cheaper stuff, and we can wait until we have enough money to buy the really good stuff that we want. This applies to everyone, whether we're rich or poor. We want to do this so that someday we can afford nice things without worrying about the cost. That all starts by sticking to our budget. It's the only way to accumulate a good nest egg to start building wealth.

Imagine you're driving a car on a road with three lanes. The middle lane is the normal and comfortable life of a regular family. The right lane is the life of the rich who can afford fancy and expensive things like a sports car. It's natural to want to be in that fast lane, but if your car isn't as fast and powerful, it's not a good idea to try to drive in that lane. You might damage your car and waste a lot of money on petrol trying to keep up with all those fast cars that have prepared themselves properly. Ultimately you will cause more damage by trying to keep up with a lifestyle you can't afford yet.

Too little, too late.

So now you know how to avoid getting into too much debt in the first place but what happens if something goes wrong? Sometimes even smart people make poor decisions. If someone does find themselves in debt, how do they get out?

This part of the journey might be hard for some people. It won't happen quickly, it will take some time. Some people might feel like they're not making progress, but if they keep working at it, they will eventually succeed. It's important to learn how to control spending before trying to pay off debt. Otherwise It's like a hamster running on a wheel - if you don't fix your spending problems, you'll never get anywhere.

Making a schedule can be really helpful when you're trying to get rid of debt, no matter how much you owe. Some people might think of schedules as strict and rigid, like being stuck in a cage. That's not the kind of schedule we're talking about. If you feel trapped, you won't want to stick with the schedule for very long. Our brains like to have some flexibility! So, how can a schedule help with debt?

Sometimes people think they will pay off their debts when they get paid, but they never actually do it. It's important to write down a plan of how much money you owe, how much you can pay back each time, and how long it will take. Writing it down makes it real and helps you remember to do it. It's okay if it takes a long time to pay off your debts, just keep trying! You can also ask the people you owe money to if they can lower the amount of interest they're charging you.

If you make a schedule to pay off your debt and stop spending money on things you don't really need, your debt will start to go away. The longer you stick to your schedule, the easier it will be to pay off your debt until one day it's all gone! It's like a big elephant that's sitting on top of you suddenly disappears into thin air!

Chapter 2.
The Ant Nest
"10 per cent rule"

Just like ants, who each bring a small amount of food back to their colony, we get paid a little bit of money with each paycheck from our first job. Even though one pay may not be enough to buy everything we want, over time all of that money will add up. It's like the ants bringing their crumbs back to the nest. They may be small on their own, but together they make a big feast for the whole colony. This is why we should try to save at least ten per cent of everything we get, so that over time we can have enough money to buy bigger things we need or want without being crushed by that pesky debt elephant. Money is useful, so we should collect little bits of it for later.

Saving money is important because it means we will have money for things we want or need in the future. It's like collecting little pieces of candy so we can eat them later when we really want them. When we save some of the money we get, we can use it to buy bigger and better things. Saving money also helps us be prepared for unexpected expenses that might happen in the future, like if we need to fix something on our first car or if we get sick and need to go to the doctor.

For every dollar we are given, we should save ten cents. For every ten dollars we are given, we should save one dollar. For every one hundred dollars we make, we should be saving at least ten dollars. Collect those little crumbs for yourself to enjoy in the future.

I went to university to study money. When I first arrived at my classes I was very eager to learn how to make buckets full of cash. I put my hand up and asked the teacher how to make a lot of money. The teacher had heard this question many times before, but had a good answer. He said to save ten cents out of every dollar we get. The ten percent rule. At first I thought my professor was an idiot. It can't be that simple but after some trial and error I realised he was correct.

When I was young I struggled to save any money at all, after following my professors rule I finally found myself with savings. I was shocked! I found out quickly that you have to save first before spending the money on other things. That's the key to being a good saver. It's like paying yourself a bill. If you spend all your money on the things you want first, you will have nothing left over each week to save. When you treat saving money like paying a bill, it becomes a powerful habit. So each payday, put money in your savings first!

When a successful person is paid money then before they do anything else, they pay themselves savings like it was a bill. If they are paid ten dollars then the first thing they do is save one dollar away for later. Unsuccessful people will usually spend the ten dollars on something they want and have nothing left to put into their savings for later.

Saving ten per cent of your money is important, but it won't make you rich by itself. There's more to it than just saving some money. Saving some money is still an important first step to becoming wealthy but it isn't where our journey ends. There's a second step to the rule that's a bit harder. Luckily it's not too complicated. The biggest challenge is actually following along because sometimes people have a hard time sticking to good habits.

The second part of the ten per cent rule is to not spend ALL your savings on flashy things. It's important to save your money even when you have a lot of it, so you can reach bigger goals like buying a house or starting a business. Sometimes people forget this and spend all their savings on things they don't really need. When someone does this, they put themselves right back to square one. This can happen because as we save our money people begin to get confident in having so much money. They forget how hard it was to have no money and they spend it all. It can be hard to remember to save, but it's worth it.

Of course It's okay to reward yourself. In fact, little rewards along the way can help encourage us to keep up those good habits. Just don't go overboard. If we go overboard and spend all of our savings on just one flashy toy then we will be back to step one. We would no longer have a safety net in case something breaks and we have to replace it. We won't have the money left to take part in great opportunities that come if we blow our savings all at once.

Have you ever really wanted something really really bad but then a week later you barely even touch it? Sometimes we might want to buy things even though we're trying to save our money. It can be hard to resist! Lucky for us there's a trick we can use to help make good choices. We can make a list of the things we want to buy, but we have to wait two weeks before buying anything on the list. This gives us time to think about whether we really want it or not. If we still want the item after a while, then we can buy it as a little treat. As long as it doesn't use up all of our savings! Most of the time, people find after they wait a week that they don't actually want to buy the thing anyway. This makes sure we don't blow our money on stupid things.

Money is useful so it makes a lot of sense to collect it over time. That doesn't just happen automatically. It is a skill we must develop. Pay yourself first.

Chapter 3.
The penguin egg
"Protecting your money"

When a female penguin lays an egg, she gives it to the male penguin to protect. The penguin puts the egg on his feet and sits there without moving until the baby penguin is ready to hatch. Through bad weather and predators, the penguin protects that egg. Protect your money even better than a penguin protects its egg. Your money is the egg you must protect so it can grow.

Unfortunately there are bad people who may lie to you in order to get your money. They may want you to sign up for something or sell you something that doesn't really help you. They do this so that the money moves from your pocket to theirs. They might say it's an amazing opportunity even if it's not great for you. It's important to think for yourself and ask if it's really good for you. This is how you protect your money.

This doesn't mean that all advice about money is bad. Sometimes the person giving you advice wants to help you. It's important to be careful and ask questions to make sure the advice is right for you. They might be making promises they can't keep. It's important to be aware of this and make smart choices with your money. Sometimes their advice might be truthful, other times it may not. You have to find honest people to trust. This is important because it helps you make better decisions. Things in life are not always going to be great all the time, so it's important to be realistic and make smart choices.

Sometimes people try to sell you things that don't make sense when you look at the numbers. Even if they tell you things will be great, it's important to be careful. Even the best investors still can't predict the future. There are some rules that good financial experts follow to make good choices. We need to be able to tell if someone is trying to sell us something or trying to help.

Asking ourselves these questions when someone is giving us advice can help:

Does the person make money if I agree?
When someone is giving advice it is important to check if they make money when you sign up to something. If they do make money then they might be motivated to give you advice that isn't right for your situation.

What have they accomplished?
Would you trust someone who isn't a mechanic to fix your mum's car? Probably not, right? It's the same with financial advice. Some people think they know everything about money, but they don't really know what they're doing at all. If someone hasn't done what you're trying to do, it is usually better not to listen to their advice.

Are they open with their failures?
When I ask for help with my money, I want someone who will tell me the truth even if things go wrong. Nobody is perfect and sometimes things don't go as planned. Honesty is important.

Is it too good to be true?
When someone tells me something that seems too good to be true, I get suspicious. If something sounds too amazing, it probably isn't real. I've always found that it is best to avoid things that are too good to be true.

Imagine that John met a man who said he could teach him how to make lots of money easily. The man asked for a small fee to join his program. He said that he could teach John to make money without doing much work.

If John uses asks himself the questions to protect himself he would find:

Does the person make money if I agree?
If he gives someone money to join their program, they get the money no matter if John himself makes money or not. It's hard to know if what they're teaching is worth it until he has paid the money. This is something to be careful about.

What have they accomplished?
Obviously not very much. They have spoken about endless money coming in from barely any work. If he had really figured that out, why would he be here selling his course to John.

Are they open with their failures?
John hasn't heard this man open up about his mistakes at all.

Is it too good to be true?
Relaxing on a beach while money comes in from doing no work at all? That type of lifestyle only comes after a lifetime of long hours of work not from simply clicking a few buttons each week.

In this case, John asking himself these questions would have saved himself a couple of hundred dollars and a bunch of time. He would protect his nest egg.

Chapter 4.
The Inflation piranha
"Why saving isn't enough"

People who have saved a lot of money often wonder what they should do with it. They might think they don't need to save anymore because they can buy nice things now. These people are wrong. If they stop being careful with their money, they will quickly find they have problems with money. It's important not to become too relaxed with our money habits. We can't assume that life will always be the same. Good savings might let us buy a few nice things but if we're not careful, we will just go around in circles.

Imagine you have an account that you put some money in. Then, you take some money out to buy something. Then, you need to put more money back in the piggy bank because you have spent some. It's like a dog trying to catch its own tail - it goes around in circles. Even if you manage to save money without spending it, there is still a problem we have to deal with. Things will get more expensive as time goes by and your money won't be worth as much. This is called inflation.

Inflation is when things get more expensive every year. In Australia, the government wants prices to go up by only two per cent each year. For most other countries, it is the same. This means that if something costs ten dollars this year, it will cost around ten dollars and twenty cents next year. This happens everywhere in the world. You might have seen this when you go to the store to buy your favourite snacks and find out that the price has gone up a little bit. This is called inflation, and it can make your money worth less over time. It's like a piranha taking bites from your money each and every year.

Let's say John saved ten dollars in the first year to buy a book, but the next year the book costs more because of inflation. If John saves ten dollars next year, he won't have enough to buy the same book he just bought this year. In fact, every year the book will get more expensive because of inflation. This means that John's money can't buy as much as it used to. Even though he saved the same amount of money, it's not worth as much anymore because of inflation.

The inflation piranha takes a two per cent bite out of money sitting in a savings account each year. Sometimes the bite is even bigger if inflation is larger during that particular year.

Every year, things cost more money because of inflation. So, if you keep your savings in a bank for a long time, it might not be enough to buy the same thing you wanted before. Even though you still have savings, it doesn't have the same power to buy things as it did before.

A long time ago, your great grandparents could buy a whole bag of candy for just one dollar. But now, one dollar can only buy one or two pieces of candy if you're lucky. Maybe even less by the time you are reading this book.

This can make it hard for people to keep up with the rising prices, even if they save their money carefully. As inflation makes things more expensive every year, a good saver will need to save more money every year just to buy the same things. This might be easy to do when it's only small amounts but adults have many expenses. As those expenses all creep up it can be hard to save. Eventually you may not have enough money to buy the things you used to be able to afford.

It is right about now that people start to hate inflation. The higher that inflation goes, the harder it is to be a good saver. Although as a customer inflation can suck, the government likes a little bit of inflation because it helps everything to grow and create more jobs. If there was no inflation, there would be no growth. No growth is terrible for both countries, investments and businesses.

On the other hand, too much of something can be bad, and inflation is no exception. When inflation is too high, it means that prices go up too quickly. It becomes hard for people to buy the things they need. This is not good for businesses either. People stop buying their products if they become too expensive, too quickly. It's important to have just the right amount of inflation, so that things can keep growing and changing, but not so much that it hurts everyone.

The government will usually step in if inflation is too low or too high, so most of the time inflation will be about two per cent. As a saver that means we are losing a little bit of our ability to buy the things we want.

The person who benefits from Inflation the most are the asset owners. The people who make investments and own businesses. This is because inflation ultimately means growth. Simply only saving won't make someone wealthy long term because the inflation piranha will swim by yearly to take a chunk out of each dollar saved. The answer is not to fight inflation and get mad. There is a system, we have to use it to our advantage. Investing in these growing businesses is the answer. We should use that inflation to our advantage. This is why simply saving is not the end of the line for becoming wealthy, it is merely a stepping stone to allow you to grow.

Chapter 5.
Time to Hunt
"Setting your aim"

Imagine there is an alligator sitting by the river waiting for a pig to come drink water. It is waiting patiently for the right moment to catch its lunch. Just like the alligator, other animals also have their own ways of finding food. Lions work together to catch prey, cheetahs chase the slowest animals, owls watch from high up in the trees for mice. All these animals have different strategies for catching food, but they all share one thing in common: they are all deliberate in their efforts

Animals don't just get lucky and randomly find food. They have a plan and know what they want to catch. For example, a crocodile doesn't accidentally come across a pig in the middle of a river. The crocodile looks for a chance to catch its food and waits patiently for it. An owl doesn't fly around hoping to find a mouse by chance. It flies to a high spot where it can see well, then searches for a mouse with its sharp eyesight.

We can learn something important from these animals who hunt for their food. Just like how they make a plan and work hard to catch their prey, we need to make a plan and work hard to make our money work for us. When we have saved a good amount of money, it's time to go hunting for opportunities to make even more money. We need to set goals and be on the lookout for chances to invest our money wisely. There are opportunities all around us, we just need to learn how to see them.

People have been using their aim to get what they want for a very long time. Long ago, people aimed their spears at animals to catch their food. They were very successful and that's why we are here today. Later on, people aimed to explore new lands and find more space. They succeeded in finding those new places. Nowadays, people aim to do things like score a goal in soccer, graduate from school, or be promoted at work. People who have a clear plan and work hard to achieve their goals are usually successful. People who don't have a plan or don't work hard usually don't do as well. Have you ever met a successful person who didn't have a plan or didn't work hard? I haven't!

Someone once said that "If you think you can do something or you think you can't do something, you're probably right". He was correct. This means that what you believe about yourself can make a big difference. If you believe you can do something, you'll be more likely to do it. If you believe you can't do something, you might not even try.

People have always aimed at things they want, like food or new places to explore. We need to do the same thing with our lives. We should focus on what we want and work towards it. It's like a lion hunting, always keeping its eyes open for its prey. We need to keep our eyes open and focus on our goals to get where we want to go.

Sometimes people want to invest their money, but they don't know how to start. When I wanted to invest my money, I had to figure out what to invest in. I thought about it for a long time because there were so many opportunities. I worked hard to save up my money, but then I learned that the money might lose its value over time because of something called inflation. So, I knew that I had to use my money to make more money.

There are many, many options for people to choose from when investing depending on their age and how much money they have access too. A few common investments are stocks and bonds. If someone has a good income and has saved well, property may also be available to them as an investment.

I had to write down what I wanted my life to look like in five years. Writing down things like having a nicer car and less money stress. I also wanted to own a business rather than work for someone else. Then I wrote down some small steps I could take to get myself closer to achieving those goals. This made the goals real and it was like a map that would guide me in the right direction.

Sometimes it can be scary to write down everything we want in life because we might not get everything we want. It's okay if we don't get everything we want straight away. The important thing is to have a direction and try our best to go in that direction. Even if we don't get everything we wanted, we will still be better off than before we started heading towards our goals.

It's important to have a goal if you want to succeed. You can't just rely on luck to get you there. So, write your goal down on a piece of paper to make it real. Even if you don't achieve everything on your list, you will still be better off than if you didn't have a goal at all. Nobody is perfect, but just trying to achieve your goals can make your life better. It's worth taking the time to write down your goals! It doesn't even have to be money related.

Chapter 6.
Stream of Salmon
"Favour cash flow"

Imagine a big, strong bear standing in a river. The river is really loud and you can hear the water flowing over the rocks. Salmon swim upstream in the river and jump out of the water. The bear waits for a salmon to jump, and then catches it in his mouth to eat. The bear doesn't try to catch all the fish at once, just one at a time. That's because he knows if he tries to catch too many fish, he might not get any at all. Just like the bear, when we are thinking about investing, it's important to have some money coming in regularly. If we don't have any money coming in, it can be really hard to keep our journey going. For most people their paycheck from their job is the cash flow they live on, however cash flow is also an important principle of a successful investment.

There are lots of ways to invest, like buying stocks, owning property or starting your own business. One thing is always important: having enough money coming in all the time. Even the best ideas won't work if you don't have enough money coming in to keep things going.

Let me tell you about buying pieces of a company. That's what some people do when they want to make more money. They buy little parts of a company by investing money in the stock market.

The stock market is a place where people can buy and sell a tiny piece of a company. Imagine you and your friends started a lemonade stand together. If you wanted to sell a tiny piece of your stand to someone else, you could do that on the stock market. If someone else wanted to buy a tiny piece of your lemonade stand, they could do that too! People can make money by buying a tiny piece of a company and then selling it later on for more money if the company does well. If the company doesn't do well, they might lose the money they invested. So, it's important to do research and make smart decisions when investing in the stock market.

The basic principle is that each stock is a claim on the businesses profits. The price for a stock in a company goes up and down based on the performance of the company and its potential profits. At different points, investors can choose to buy or sell the stock depending on the price.

Pretend that Kerry is interested in investing her money in the stock market. She has two investment options. She has one thousand dollars to invest. Company 1 has been growing really fast and Kerry thinks it will continue to grow. Company 2 has been growing more slowly but it pays money every month to the people who invest in it.

Kerry thinks she will sell her stock at the end of the year and use the extra money for a holiday. This is a short amount of time for an investment so she probably won't make too much money. Most investments need a long time to pay off. Luckily for all of us, this is a book and we can fast forward one year to see what would have happened to each investment.

If she picked Company 1 and put in a thousand dollars, After one year, she could sell the stock for eleven hundred dollars. That means she made one hundred dollars more than what she started with! That is a ten per cent gain. The price of the stock went up because the company is growing fast. Pretty impressive for only a year!

If Kerry invested in Company 2, at the end of the year she would sell the stock for one thousand and fifty dollars, however, she received a total of an extra fifty dollars worth of payments from the company throughout the year. These payments are called dividends. Dividends are a share in the profits that a company gives to people who own their stock. If you own a company's stock, it means you have a little piece of that company. So when the company makes a lot of money, they may distribute it.

At the end of the year, Kerry would make the same amount of money from both stocks but there's a difference. One stock grew a lot and the other didn't grow as much. Instead It gave Kerry dividends throughout the year. Even though Kerry would make the same amount of money from both stocks, she would make it in different ways. So is one investment better than the other?

We talked about how things can get more expensive over time because of inflation. When Kerry gets money from the dividends, it's like getting a little bit of extra money before everything gets more expensive. She can use that money to buy something now or save it for later. She may even choose to reinvest it. If Kerry invests in company 1, she only gets all her money at the end of the year when the inflation piranha has already taken a bite out of her money. Investing in company 2 gives her more options to use some of her money before inflation takes hold because she receives the money earlier.

Cash flow is also so important for new investors because unexpected expenses happen and we need to have some money to pay for them. For example, when my first car broke down, I had to pay to get it fixed. If I had money coming in regularly, it would be easier to handle these expenses without getting too stressed out. If I had to wait a long time before receiving any money, I would be without a car for a while. Even worse, I may have had to sell my investment for a loss. No one ever expects things to go wrong but sometimes in life, they do. Favouring investments that are cash flow positive helps us deal with those unexpected expenses.

These unexpected expenses are called "economic shocks". When we invest, it's good to get money back along the way instead of only at the very end.

That way, if something unexpected happens, we can use the money from the investment to pay for it. We can also decide if we want to use the money to buy something else or put it back into investing. If we have to wait a long time to get our money back from an investment, we might have to sell it early if we have too many unexpected bills to pay. Selling investments early often means you lose money.

It is because of these economic shocks and the inflation piranha that money now is often better than money later.

Chapter 7.
Collect all the fruit
"Hoard assets and play monopoly"

There's a little monkey in Bali that likes to take things from tourists. If you get too close to their trees, they might steal your things like your camera or wallet. These monkeys are really smart and know that people will want their things back. These monkeys only give them back if they get something they want in return. These monkeys have learned that it's good to keep things that will benefit them. They hold onto valuable things.

Have you ever played a board game where you buy properties and charge rent to other players? It can be a lot of fun, but sometimes one person can buy too many properties and become too powerful. We can learn a lot from this game. The main idea is to keep things that make you money and don't sell them too quickly. Just like in the game, holding on to the things that make you money can help you build your wealth over time.

Margaret owns a shop and another shop owner named Peter wants to sell his business and retire. Peter's shop is larger than Margarets. Margaret could either say no and miss a good opportunity or buy Peter's business and make more money. If Margaret buys Peter's business, she can buy items for the shops in bulk for a cheaper price. She would also get new customers from a different area of town. Margaret doesn't want to sell her current laundromat because it's doing well. Margaret talks with some experts to make a proposal to buy Peter's business. She gives Peter half the money at first and pays the rest later with the profits from both laundromats. After some changes to the proposal, Peter agrees to sell his business to Margaret. Now Margaret has two laundromats and her business is better.

This is a smart decision because Margaret kept her money making assets. Her original shop made a few thousand dollars a week and her new shop that she purchased off of Peter makes much more than that. She was smart to keep both stores and combine the incomes of both whilst being able to reduce her costs. If she hadn't saved her money so well, this would never be possible.

What about Peter? Should he have sold his shop? Peter wanted to retire and enjoy his life, but he had a business that he needed to take care of. He had two choices: he could sell the business and get a lot of money up front, but then over time he risks running out of money.

Instead he could have hired an employee and although his profits would be smaller because he is paying an employee, he would still have money coming into his bank account permanently. Peter chose to sell his business to Margaret, but that might not have been the best choice. If he runs out of money, he might have to ask the government or family for help. It's important to be able to take care of yourself when you're older and not have to rely on anyone else.

Let me explain it to you like this. We all use money to buy things we need and want. Life can be very expensive, and it's something that people start to realise when they become adults. Everyday adults have to spend money on food and bills. Peter sold his business so now he has lots of money in his account but no more money will be coming in. What he has is the last of his money. Over time, he will pay his bills and eat his food. Every week the money in Peter's bank account will get smaller and smaller because he has no cash coming inwards. It's only a matter of time before Peter runs out of money and is broke. Especially as inflation eats away at his money over the years on top of all his regular bills.

Wealthy people know to hoard the assets that make them money, just like those monkeys in Bali know to hang onto the things they can swap for food.

I have a cousin who is really good at saving money and investing it. She and her husband worked really hard and owned a café. They used the money from the café to buy two little houses, which they rented out to people for extra money. They lived very cheap and were able to pay off their debts quickly. Then they used the money they made from the houses and the café to buy more businesses that made them even more money. They never sold any of their money making assets, they just kept buying more things that made them more money. An asset is something that you own that is valuable and can help you make money. Basically it is something that brings money inwards. The rich and wealthy hold onto these assets.

It was hard work for my cousin, but they never gave up. Now, they have a lot of money and lots of nice things like fancy cars, boats and toys. They're doing really well and people around them wonder how they did it. They just saved and invested their money smartly. They treated it like they were playing a board game and now they own most of the property on the board.

My cousin was able to grab so many assets on the board because she reinvested so well. Reinvesting means using the money your investments made to buy things that will make you even more money in the future. This can be slow at first but speeds up the more you do it. Ultimately this is how you outrun inflation. Someone who has reinvested heavily will have many assets. Someone who hasn't reinvested will struggle to grow their kingdom as quickly because each year the inflation piranha is eating away at their empire.

Chapter 8.
Seasons of an economy
"Understanding the economic seasons"

An economy is like a big game that people play to buy and sell things they need or want. Just like how you might play a game with your friends online, in an economy, people trade things like food, cars, clothes, and toys. The economy is like a big group of people playing a game together. Just like in any game, there are rules that everyone has to follow, so that it's fair for everyone. When the economy is doing well, people have enough of what they need and they can buy more of the things they want. When the economy is not doing well, people might not have enough money to buy everything they need or want. Every country has an economy and almost all adults play a part in an economy.

We have four seasons of the year, we also have different seasons in our economy. The way people spend and make money changes over this cycle. People who wear fancy suits call this the economic cycle. We can think about the economic cycle like the weather outside. It affects how much money everyone has and how much everything costs.

Outside we experience the weather as Summer then Autumn, Winter and Spring. There is an order to it. Unlike the weather, the economic seasons can happen in any order. Each season has its own characteristics, kind of like how summer is hot and sunny, and winter is cold and sometimes snowy. If we can understand the signs of the economic seasons, we can be better prepared for what might happen with everyones money in the future.

When the economy is in an expansion period, things are growing and getting bigger. This means more people have jobs and are making more money. You might also notice that things start to cost more. If you hear people talking about how more people are getting jobs or making more money, it could be a sign that we are in an expansion season.

A recession is the opposite of the time when things are growing and expanding. This is just like how winter is the opposite of summer. During a recession, things in the economy slow down. Prices start to fall and people may lose their jobs. It can be harder for businesses to sell their products or services during this time. Some people might call it an "economic slowdown."

A boom period is like a really, really hot day in summer. The economy gets so hot that it's overheating. During a boom, lots of people get paid more money at their jobs and the stock market rises really quickly. Things can get too hot and go wrong. Sometimes, things get so hot that the prices of things, like houses, go up too much and people can't afford them anymore. So we have to be careful during a boom period not to get burnt.

A depression is when the economy is doing very, very badly. It's like the worst kind of winter storm you can think of. People don't have enough jobs, so they don't have enough money to buy things. This makes it hard for stores to sell things, so they lower their prices. This makes it harder for the stores to make money so they begin to fire people from their jobs. This can make it very hard for families to have enough money to buy the things they need to live.

A peak in the market means it's the highest point of good times in the economy. Some people try to guess when this will happen, but it's really hard to predict correctly. Don't believe anyone who tries to make you pay money for a secret trick to know when the peak is going to happen.

A trough is when the economy is at the very bottom of a bad time. Some people try to guess when it will hit the very bottom so they can buy things when they're cheap. This is very hard to do and usually doesn't work out. Catching a falling knife is dangerous.

Even when things are not going well in the economy, people can still make money. I like to check the economic news a few times a year to see what season we are in. This helps me understand if things are getting better or worse, and I can use this information to decide which companies to invest in the stock market. This way, even if the economy is not doing well, I can still make money.

Unfortunately there are no concrete rules but a bit of common sense goes a long way. Different types of businesses perform differently during different economic seasons. For example, when people don't have jobs or money, they can't buy really expensive things so it's best to avoid luxury businesses when times are tough. People still need to eat, so companies that sell basic foods like rice and pasta usually do okay during tough times. When things are tough, people usually stop doing fun things like going to the cinema or theme parks, so entertainment companies might not do so well. With so many companies to choose from on the stock market, it can be hard to know which ones to invest in, but understanding the economic seasons can help investors make good choices. Ask yourself, how would different types of businesses do in each season? That's a good step in understanding how the economy affects the stock market.

Different people have different reasons for buying stocks. Some people buy them to save money for retirement, while others buy them to make money in the long term. When the government changes the rules or something happens in the economy, people start to sell their stocks or buy new ones. This causes the prices of stocks to go up or down. It's kind of like a game where everyone is trying to make money. It's important to pay attention to what's happening in the economy so that you don't make a mistake and lose money when investing.

Chapter 9.
The Tallest Tree
"Dollar-cost averaging"

The tallest tree in the forest has stood tall through
the sun, wind, frost, rain and hail. It has survived
droughts, bushfires and the harshest weather
nature has to throw at it. Standing tall
during flooding and downpours, the tallest trees are
affected by the conditions around them but
not ruined by them. The tallest trees are able to
weather all storms.

Despite all of this, tall trees in the forest grow
differently when the weather is different. Our money
can also grow differently when the economy
changes. Sometimes our money grows quickly, and
other times it doesn't grow much at all.

It is always important to remember that it is very
hard to find the perfect time to invest. Some people
think they can predict when to invest their money in
the stock market, but it's impossible to be right all
the time. They try to use news and their feelings to
figure out when to buy and sell, but it's rarely

accurate. Some people say they know how to make a lot of money by investing at the right time, but even the professionals struggle to do it consistently.

Imagine you wanted to grow a lemon tree. You wouldn't be able to get lemons right away, you'd have to wait for the tree to grow and get bigger. Investing in the stock market is kind of like growing a tree. Growth takes time. If you keep taking your money out and putting it back in all the time, you'll end up losing money because you have to pay extra fees every time you buy and sell. So, it's better to just let your money grow over time in solid investments rather than small opportunities. Time in the market is more important than trying to pick the best time to invest. Let me say that again. Time in the market is more important than timing the market.

Sometimes people might feel scared to invest because they don't know when it's a good time to buy. This is common for first time investors. They worry they might buy something and then the price will decline. Nobody can know for sure when the price will go up or down. So instead of trying to time it perfectly, there is a way to buy investments that many people use called dollar-cost averaging. It's an easy way to buy investments a little bit at a time instead of all at once.

Instead of trying to be lucky and buy at the perfect time, it's better to buy a little bit at a time over a long time. If we buy good things, they will grow in value over time. We need to be patient, just like how we wait for our lemon tree to grow and give us lemons. The exact price we buy at doesn't matter too much. What matters is how long we keep it for and buying little bits over time will mean we aren't buying the investment right before it will crash or right before it is about to take off like a rocket. Instead dollar-cost averaging means that investors will get the price in the middle over time which is perfect for someone who is holding long term.

Big trees take a long time to grow. They don't grow overnight. When investing It's easy to let our feelings control us but we should try to avoid rushing into anything. The dollar-cost strategy means that our excitement won't get ahead of us.

When we invest using this method, we don't have to worry so much about how we feel at any one time. Sometimes people get too excited and buy an investment without thinking enough. Other times people get too scared and sell an investment too quickly. With dollar-cost averaging, we make smaller investments regularly over a period of time, so we're less likely to make mistakes based on our emotions. This can help us avoid losing money we don't need to lose.

Another benefit of this method is that we can buy stocks at lower prices over a long time. When the market goes down, some people panic and sell their investments when they don't need to. With dollar-cost averaging, we keep buying the stock even when the price is lower. This can help us reduce our costs in the long run.

If an investor did their research into a company and decided that they are worth investing into, using the dollar cost average method they wouldn't buy all their shares straight away. If they had two thousand dollars to invest, they might buy four lots of five hundred dollars worth over the next four months. Over those four months, the price will fluctuate up and down but these small fluctuations likely won't matter in ten years time if the investor was right about the company in the first place.

Dollar-cost averaging is when you decide to buy an asset, like a stock or a share of a company, at regular times no matter what the price is. It's not about trying to buy at the lowest price or the highest price, but just buying at the same time intervals. You could decide to buy every two weeks or every month or even once a year. It doesn't matter how long you do it for, as long as you stick to the same time intervals. The point is to avoid becoming emotional when investing.

Whilst it is a good strategy, but it does not always guarantee we will make money. If we choose a bad investment, we may lose money even if we use this strategy. However, if we choose a good investment, we can make money in the long run. It could be risky if the asset you invest in is not a good one. For example, if the company you buy stocks from is going to go bankrupt, then you will lose your money. This is true for all types of investments, not just stocks on a stock market.

Chapter 10.
Fresh fruit, rotten fruit
"Bad vs Good debt"

Earlier in the book we spoke about debt. As a teen you won't have much debt. Banks won't loan you money when you are so young. It's not something you have to worry about right now. As you grow up though, you will find yourself dealing with debt a bit more. Whether it is a potential car loan, or student loans, you will eventually encounter debt. When people owe money to others, it can make their life very hard. Not all money that people owe is the same. Some kinds of debt are good, like fresh fruit that helps us grow and be strong. Other debts are bad, like rotten fruit that makes us sick. We can use good debt to help us grow and improve our lives but if we eat the bad debt, it will only hurt us and make things worse. So what makes one debt good and another bad?

Good debt is a type of loan that can help you make more money. You can use it to buy things that make money for you. A loan to buy an asset that brings money inwards can be good debt.

Bad debt is when you borrow money to buy things that don't help you make more money. These things may not last long and their value may go down over time. This type of debt makes you poorer because you have to pay for them and it doesn't help you get more money. Bed debt is often made up mostly of luxury items.

Good debt increases the money coming into your bank and bad debt takes money out of your bank. Good debt can help investors grow their kingdom much faster but it is still risky. Good debts can become bad debts. For example, a loan to buy a business might be a good idea but it can go badly. There are no guarantees that business or investment will pay off well enough to pay off the debt.

Good debt can be helpful when used wisely to grow your wealth, but always remember that it still has some risk. Sometimes people take on good debt for things like education or starting a business, but those things may not work out and the debt can become bad. The point of good debt is to help you grow, but it's not totally safe. Whilst you are young you shouldn't worry too much about debt at all. Only that you shouldn't fall into the trap of putting expensive luxury toys onto a credit card. As you grow, it is just as important to remember that not all debt is bad debt.

Bad debt is much more obvious to spot than good debt. Almost all consumer debt is bad. Luxury items like sunglasses, designer clothes and everything alike only take money out of your bank account. Anyone using debt to buy things like this is making themselves worse off.

Chapter 11.
Lending to the tribe
"The bond market"

A long time ago, people found a way to borrow and lend things to each other. We don't know exactly who the first person to borrow and lend was. Maybe it was a caveman borrowing someone else's spear while they were hunting. This kind of borrowing and lending has been happening for thousands of years. It helped people to build civilizations and become rich. We are all probably familiar with borrowing things but lending is the other side of the equation.

When someone borrows money, there has to be someone else who gives them the money. We call the person who gives the money the lender. The person who takes it is the borrower. You have probably borrowed money before. Have you ever thought about what it's like to be the person who lends the money? It's not something everyone does, but certain investors cangive money to others and expect them to pay it back with extra money called interest.

A bond is like a small loan that someone can buy. It's called a bond because it's an agreement that bonds two people. One person lends money to another person who promises to pay it back later with extra money as interest. The bond market is where people go to buy and sell these agreements.

There are two types of bonds: government bonds and private bonds. When you buy a government bond, you're lending money to the government. When you buy a private bond, you're lending money to a company. The amount of extra money you get back is called the yield. The higher the yield, the more money you make.

When a company wants to build a new factory or the government wants to build a new road, the money has to come from somewhere. So they can ask investors to lend them money by buying something called a bond.

A bond is like a special paper that says the company or government will borrow a certain amount of money from you. They promise to pay you back the money you lent them plus a little bit extra.

Let's say the company needs ten thousand dollars to build a new factory. They decide to make ten bonds, each worth one thousand dollars. They promise to pay back the money in a certain number of years, and they'll pay a certain amount of interest to the people who bought the bonds. Investors can choose to buy one or more of the company's bonds and lend them the money they need. Over time, the company pays back the money plus interest to the investors. If the investor chooses to, they can sell these bonds to other investors. In modern times the bond market and stock market have become very similar.

Although bonds roughly all work the same, not all bonds are the same. Some are more risky than others. Even bonds from governments can be risky and are not always safe. Some countries have borrowed money from people and never paid it back. The same thing can happen with companies. Some company bonds are very risky while others are less risky, depending on what the company is doing with the money. No bond or investment is completely safe, so there is always some risk involved for the person investing their money.

For example, if a company wants to build a new department in their shop that will make a lot of money, it's less risky to loan them money than if they were trying to build a rocket to go to the moon. This is because we know that building a bigger shop is more likely to make money than some wild adventure. When it comes to bond investing, the most important thing to know is whether the company or government will be able to pay back the loan.

We know that there are always risks with investing, but the bond market is often less risky than buying stocks or property. This is because an investor can see what return they will get from the start. If an investor puts their money in the stock market, they won't know for certain how much money they might get back. If a person buys stock on the stock market in a company building a new shop they have no way of knowing how much money they will make from buying that stock. If instead, the investor uses a bond to help that business build a new shop, the investor will already have agreed on the yield before ever investing. That yield is their return. This is much more certain than buying a stock. When an investor buys a bond they can see the interest that they will receive from the bond from the very start.

Chapter 12.
Building Shelters
"The property market"

Animals, like birds, beavers, and rabbits, build their homes in different ways. Some collect sticks and twigs, some bite and chop trees, and some dig holes in the dirt. Humans also need homes, and we hire people to build them for us. Everyone needs a safe place to live, and as more people are born, we need more homes for everyone. There are lots of different types of homes. Big ones, Small ones and funny shaped ones. People have been building homes for a really long time. When we talk about property, we usually think about the places we live, but owning a home is different than owning something that makes you money. Owning a home is important because it keeps you safe and gives you a place to live, but it doesn't make any money for you. When you buy a home, no money comes into your bank, money only flows outwards. your home itself is not an asset.

A property is an investment when it brings the owner income. This can happen when they rent out the property to someone else. That person will pay the owner to use the space. A property might also be an investment if someone was going to repair it quickly and sell it for more than they originally paid. Land can also be a property investment if there is going to be something built on top of it to be sold off for a profit.

When we talk about investing in property, we mean buying a property that will make us money. Sometimes people buy a property just because they want to use it themselves, like a vacation home. That's okay, but it doesn't make it an investment. To be a good property investor, you need to plan and do research. The research itself is not very hard but it is important. Some people make a lot of money from investing in property and can even make a career out of it.

Throughout history, the people who have been very rich are the ones who own the land. Think about a big city with big buildings and shops. Someone owns all of those buildings, and that brings them buckets full of money. This all started with someone deciding to invest in property.

It can be very very expensive to start property investing. Many adults struggle to afford to invest this way. Much like many other investments, cash flow is king for success in property. If you want to buy land and wait for it to become more valuable, you need money to pay for things while you wait. If you want to fix up a property and sell it for more money, you need money to pay for the repairs. If you want to build a new property, you need money to pay for the building. If you want to rent out a property, you need money to pay for things like repairs to the house. These are just some of the reasons why property investment can be expensive. So, it's really important that property investors make sure you have enough money to start off with.

When someone makes a property investment, they can be divided into two types. Housing and commercial. Housing is where people live, while commercial is where businesses operate. When we think about property, most people think about houses. People usually start by investing in housing because it's easier to understand. Commercial property is more complicated because there are different rules than housing. However, some people prefer commercial property because the prices are not as affected by the same things as residential housing. Whilst property prices can be affected by things like access to schools and hospitals nearby, this is not the case for commercial property. prices often depend on how much business is going on in the area rather than the population demographics.

Regardless of what type of property investors pick, property investment often comes later on in life. This is because it is so very expensive. It's much cheaper to buy a stock or bond than it is to buy a house.

Chapter 13.
Wind in a sail
Interest rates and their effects

Long ago, people used the wind to explore new places and find new lands. They made big boats from trees and floated down rivers. Later, they made boats with sails and went out into the big ocean. The wind would blow the boat in different directions and sailors learned how to use it to their advantage. Just like the sailors, we can use the wind, or something called the interest rate, to help us grow our money. It might take some time to learn, but we can use it to help us buy things like stocks, property, and bonds.

Interest rates control the cost of borrowing money. Interest rates can also affect how much money you can earn from your savings account. If the interest rate is high, you can earn more money from your savings, but if it's low, you will earn less. The government sets the country's main interest rate to help control things like unemployment and inflation. The rate will go up and down throughout the year as the government tries to achieve the best balance for the economy.

The government cares about interest rates because they can use them to control how much money people spend. When interest rates go down, people can spend more money because they pay less on their loans. When interest rates go up, people have to pay more on their loans and have less money to spend. Almost everyone that owns a home has a mortgage of some sort so these changes affect a lot of people at once. Changing levels of spending helps the government control things like the employment rate and inflation. This also affects ways of investing your money differently.

The stock market is tricky and changes all the time. Even though we can't always predict what will happen, we know that when interest rates go up, people spend less money. We know that when interest rates go down, people spend more money. Some companies rely heavily on people having money to spend on luxuries. When interest rates are low, the government wants people to spend more money and retail companies may do well. When interest rates go up, the government wants people to spend less money and some companies may not do as well. For example, if the government lowers interest rates and more people buy TVs, the company that makes the TVs might do well and their stock might go up.

Investors will move their money around the stock market to where they think people will be spending their money in the economy. The more people who sell their stock in a company, the more the price of that company should go down. The more people buy stock in a company, the more the price should go up.

Understanding interest rates can help us predict how people will spend their money. When the government raises interest rates, people have less money to spend and may be less likely to buy expensive things like luxury cars. On the other hand, when interest rates are low, people may be more likely to take out loans and buy things they can't afford, like cars. We can use this knowledge to make smart decisions about buying stocks. It is much easier to see how changes in the interest rate will affect property investors. The interest rate affects how much it will cost to buy a property.

Almost everyone will need a mortgage to buy a property and so they must pay interest. When the interest rate is low, people have to pay less in repayments each month for their property. When it is high, they have to pay more money back each month.

When the interest rate is high, some people might not have enough money to pay for a loan to buy a house, so they will wait to buy one. When the interest rate is low, more people can afford to buy a house and so more people try to buy one. When there are a lot of people trying to buy a house, the price might go up. When not many people want to buy a house, the price might go down. This is because there needs to be a balance between buyers and sellers. When there are more buyers, there should be a price rise. When there are more sellers, there should be a price drop.

The effect that interest rate changes have on the bond market is a bit more tricky to understand. If the interest rate goes up, investors are **less** likely to want older bonds because those bonds still have the lower interest rate. Why would anyone want to make a lesser return for the same cost? Instead, the newer bonds will be highly desired by investors and they may ignore the older bonds. This might mean those older bonds will sell for less and the newer ones will sell for more. The same is true in reverse. If interest rates go down, Why would an investor want to buy new bonds with a low rate?

Instead they might want the older bonds with the better return. Although that might be tricky to understand, the key thing to remember is that buyers will chase the higher yield bonds when everything else stays the same.

Chapter 14.
Leap out of the nest
"Risk Management"

Every little birdie has to leave the nest and learn to fly eventually. It takes weeks of getting strong and making its feathers perfect. When the time is right, it has to take a big leap of faith and fly for the first time. The first flight is really dangerous, even if the bird has prepared. Despite the danger, it's important for the bird to fly because that's what birds are meant to do.

Life is full of risks. Bad things can happen to anyone. Every day, we face risks when we go outside. There are risks even if we hide away at home. It isn't possible to be risk free in life. Risk is all around us, but we don't need to be terrified of it. We can't make everything safe, no matter how hard we try. So, instead of being too cautious or trying to make everything safe, we need to learn how to deal with risk in a healthy way. We need to manage our risk.

It is pretty common for people to have a bad relationship with risk. Some of these people could be called the "cowboy" because they take too many risks and don't plan ahead. They think that since there are risks in life anyway, they might as well do whatever they want. They take risks for fun. The cowboy doesn't think about what could go wrong and doesn't have backup plans. This is not safe.

The other type of person with a poor relationship with risk is called the "worried parent". They worry too much and try to avoid risks altogether. They are afraid of everything and wrap themselves in bubble wrap. They miss out on fun experiences because they are too scared to try anything new. This is also not a good way to live.

Both the cowboy and the worried parent are dangerous in their own way. The cowboy can get into trouble because they take too many risks without thinking. The worried parent misses out on life because they are too afraid to take any risks.

It's important to find a balance between taking risks and being safe. Having a healthy relationship with risk doesn't mean being super reckless or super scared all the time. It means walking in the middle and making reasonable choices.

Risk means different things to different people depending on the situation. When we talk about managing risk, we mean managing the risks involved in investing. When we Invest we are using our money to buy something in the hope that it will make more money in the future. Sometimes it doesn't work out and you can lose your money for a number of reasons. There are many risks that investors face, like having to pay more fees or needing special permission to make certain investments. Investors can manage these risks so they don't get too hurt. There are three main ways to do this.

Have you ever heard of "beta risk"? It's something that people learn about in university when they study finance. It might seem hard to understand, but don't worry, we will simplify it. Beta is just a special way of looking at risk and figuring out how risky an investment might be. You can even use it in everyday life.

The price of something changes depending on how many people want to buy and sell it. If there is a lot of something and not many people want it, the price will be low. If there is only a little bit of something and lots of people want it, the price will be high. Beta risk says that the more the price fluctuates, the riskier the asset is. The more the price goes up and down, the riskier it is.

Investors need to care about variation in price because it affects how much money they can make when they sell their investment. If the price changes a lot, it can be hard to predict how much money you will get if and when you sell your investment. This makes it risky because investors might sell at a bad time and lose money. An asset that has a price that moves up and down a lot less makes it easier to predict how much the investor will really get for their asset. If the price of apples is one dollar today but yesterday it was three dollars and tomorrow it will be ten dollars, is that a very stable investment? Probably not when we compare it to a banana that stayed the same price the whole time. Stability is what investors look for when trying to reduce their risk.

Macro risks are the big picture things that can go wrong when you invest in something. If you buy a car wash, you need to make sure the machines are working well and are not broken. If you want to build apartments, you need to make sure you have permission from the government and that people want to live in the area. These things might sound scary, but they don't mean you shouldn't invest. You just need to think about how you can solve these problems and if your investment is likely to do well. Each investment is different, so you need to think about what could go wrong and if you can fix it. Understanding each investment in detail is the best way to reduce this type of risk.

Don't put all your eggs in one basket, my grandmother used to tell me. Exposure risk is all about making sure you don't lose all your money when you invest. There are two main ways investors can be at risk of losing money. They can invest too much in one place or by investing too much in one type of business. When investors place all their money into one investment, only one thing needs to go wrong for it to be game over. Always keep an eye on how much money you have invested in the market and to spread your money across different types of businesses so that you don't lose everything if one type of investment doesn't do well. Never invest more than you can afford to lose. To keep their money safe, investors can diversify. Having many investments means less risk when something goes wrong.

Chapter 15.
Fall out of the tree sometimes
"Be okay with failure"

Failure is important. Even baby lions miss their prey the first time. They need to learn and practice. They watch and try again and again, even if they fail. Over time, they become better and better, until they are the kings or queens of the jungle. This is true for almost every animal in the world. Many grown-up people are afraid of failing and don't want to try. We can't be perfect right away. To become better at things, we need to learn from our mistakes. That means that we first have to make mistakes.

We can read to learn a lot about money and investing, but the best way to get good at something is to get your hands dirty. Just like when you play a sport or a game, you need to practise and make mistakes before you can get any good. It's the same with money. Everyone will make mistakes along the way, but that's okay because it helps us learn and get better. So, don't be afraid to try and don't worry if you don't get it right the first time. You don't have to be great at saving money straight away, it takes practice. Most first time investors lose some money to begin with. It's all a learning process.

Building wealth can be tricky, and it's okay if you make mistakes. Even when you do everything right, sometimes things don't work out. Saving money, buying stocks, and paying off debts all have risks. Sometimes things will go well, but sometimes they won't. It is important to keep trying and not give up, even when you fail. When people get discouraged and give up too soon, they won't be successful. You have to be okay with making mistakes sometimes to be successful in building your own Wealth Kingdom.

Building wealth is like building a tower with blocks. You need to take many steps to build it up, but sometimes you may make a mistake and the tower falls down. That's okay because you can try again and build it up even taller. Some people know how to build the tower really well, but they are too scared to try. They are afraid they will make a mistake and the tower will fall. If they don't try, they will never build a tower at all. Giving up or never starting to begin with means you will never build a tower. It's important to keep trying, even if you make mistakes along the way.

When we try to achieve our goals again, we have more knowledge to help us be successful. We get this knowledge from being honest about our failures. When things go wrong, it is important to figure out what we did wrong. This means we need to take some time to think about what we did and be truthful about it. Did we manage our risks? Did we save our money first? Did we use bad debt? All these things can derail our success but being honest reflection can bring us back onto the right path.

If I feel like I have failed to reach one of my goals, I ask myself the same questions every time. I define failure by clearly asking myself what exactly went wrong. I get really specific why my plan to reach my goal didn't work. I ask myself why I failed? Did I manage my risks or did I plan wrong? This leads to myself asking what could I do better next time? It's true sometimes things just go wrong but could I have done something better. All these questions help me understand why I missed my goal and how I can achieve it next time.

This book talks about making and having lots of money, but money isn't the only way to be happy or successful. Spending time with family and being a good person are also important. Sometimes people make decisions that bring them a lot of money, but they might miss out on important things with their family or friends. Success with money doesn't mean anything if you have missed out on life and loved ones.

People make mistakes and fail, but that's okay. As long as you keep trying and don't give up, it's okay to fail sometimes. You just have to get back up and try again.